OMG! Thoughts Become Things!

The Blue Bear Family on The Law of Thinking

Grace B. Simmons, Ph.D.

Illustrated by Donovan Brown and Grace A. Simmons

Archway Publishing books may be ordered through booksellers or by contacting:

Archway Publishing
1663 Liberty Drive
Bloomington, IN 47403
www.archwaypublishing.com
844-669-3957

ISBN: 978-1-6657-2722-8 (sc)
ISBN: 978-1-6657-2723-5 (hc)
ISBN: 978-1-6657-2724-2 (e)

Print information available on the last page.

Archway Publishing rev. date: 08/26/2022

Inspired by Raymond Holliwell's, Working with The Law,
in conjunction with Mary Morrissey and Bob Proctor

Look around you. What do you see?
Everything you see was created twice
First in someone's thoughts
And then in their life.

Look at your life. What do you see?
Everything you see was created twice
First, through the thoughts that you spent a lot of time thinking about
And then, by those things becoming real visible things in your life.

Whatever you plant in your mind
Is what will grow in your life
Whether it's thoughts of love and happiness
Or thoughts of things that are not nice.

Your thoughts are powerful things
Why not use them to feed your imagination
To create the life that you would truly love to live
Or to produce some new sensation?

If you think about this seriously
You will find this to be true
In life, the thoughts that you've been thinking
Are the things that come back to you.

Your thoughts become your things
And your things are a result of your thoughts
Therefore, you are the one responsible
For your life's results.

Your mind is like a garden
And your thoughts are like the seeds
Your good thoughts bring you flowers
While your bad thoughts bring you weeds.

If things are not going
The way you want them to go
Change the seeds that you plant
Change the thoughts that you sow.

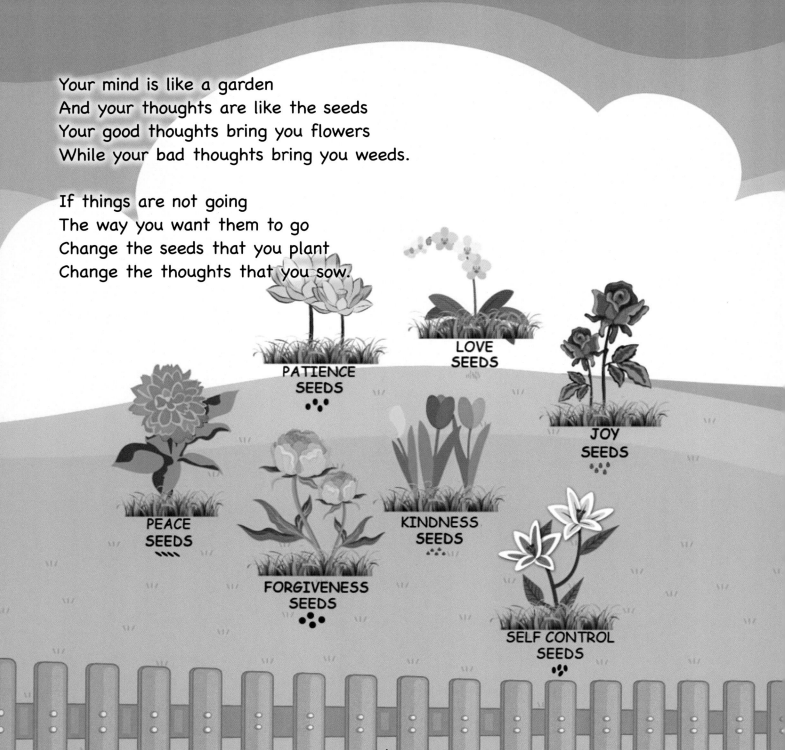

PATIENCE
SEEDS

LOVE
SEEDS

JOY
SEEDS

PEACE
SEEDS

FORGIVENESS
SEEDS

KINDNESS
SEEDS

SELF CONTROL
SEEDS

Watch carefully the thoughts
That you allow yourself to think
They can either cause you to soar in life
Or they can cause you to sink.

Since your thoughts become things
You might ask, what are you to do?
Just put on the right thoughts
Like you put on your shoe?

NEGATIVE THOUGHTS

5

Don't think about the things that you don't want
Think about the things that you do
So that the pictures that are etched in your mind
Will produce the things that you want for you.

To get rid of the darkness
You don't have to chase it away
Just turn on the light
And the darkness cannot stay.

LIGHT
SWITCH

7

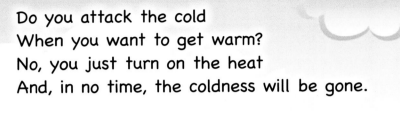

Do you attack the cold
When you want to get warm?
No, you just turn on the heat
And, in no time, the coldness will be gone.

Likewise, don't fight with negative thoughts
When they appear in your mind
Just replace them with positive ones
And do that every time!

LOOK FOR THE POSSIBLE GOOD IN EVERYONE AND EVERY SITUATION.

You must focus, focus, focus
On what you truly desire
And visualize it so spectacularly
That it sets your heart on fire!

Focusing, visualizing, imagining
Will choke out the other thoughts
Because your attention will be laser focused
On creating your desired results.

9

For every seed that's planted
There is a germination period
It's the same when you plant thoughts
Belief and patience are the criteria.

Thinking with strong emotions
Will yield the best results.
The more enthusiastic you are
The more powerful your thoughts!

NOTHING CAN STOP US NOW!
IF WE FALL DOWN, WE WILL SIMPLY
GET BACK UP AND TRY AGAIN!

You may need some help
When trying to leave unpleasant things behind
Try talking to someone you trust
Or draw or write about what's on your mind.

Then release the situation
Trust God to work it out for your good
I know that He will do it
Because He promised that He would!

Whatever is good
True, lovely, and kind
Those are the things
That you should feed your mind!

And take little baby steps daily
Towards your dream
It's a whole lot easier
Than what it might seem.

EACH DAY WE WILL
DO SOME THING THAT
WILL TAKE US CLOSER
TO OUR DREAMS, EVEN
IF IT'S ONLY JUST
THINKING ABOUT IT.

GOALS

		1	2	3	4	5	6
7	8	9	10	11	12	13
14	15	16	17	18	19	20
21	22	23	24	25	26	27
28	29	30	31			

CALENDAR

You can be anything
That you truly want to be.
Nothing is impossible
If the impossible you can see!

You are here by Divine permission
You are not here by accident!
You are on a special mission
That is why you have been sent!

An engineer, a singer
An attorney, a teacher
A physician, an entrepreneur
An athlete, a preacher.

An honor student, homemaker
A designer, an artist
Whatever would make you happy
You don't have to be the smartest!

From the clothes that you're wearing
To the technology online
They all were first thoughts
Created in somebody's mind.

The type of house in which you live
The automobile in which you ride
The things that you enjoy
From the smartphone to the slide.

From the great pyramids in Egypt
To the majestic towering Sphinx
From the furniture in your house
To the design of skating rinks.

These things were all thoughts
Before they were designed
By someone like you
With an idea in their mind.

OPEN YOUR MINDS TO THE
UNLIMITED FLOW OF POSITIVE
THOUGHTS AND IDEAS AND
IMAGINE!!!

Grace B. Simmons, PhD is a retired educator with forty-two years of experience as a teacher, dropout prevention coordinator, and school counselor. She is a former national sales director and Christian education district director who holds a bachelor's degree in elementary education, a master's degree in school counseling, and a doctorate in Christian counseling. Dr. Simmons is a Certified DreamBuilder Consultant, a pastor's wife, mother, and grandmother.

Printed in the United States
by Baker & Taylor Publisher Services